Extreme Laboratories

ANN O. SQUIRE

Children's Press®
An Imprint of Scholastic Inc.
New York   Toronto   London   Auckland   Sydney
Mexico City   New Delhi   Hong Kong
Danbury, Connecticut

Content Editor
Robert Wolffe, EdD
Professor, Bradley University
Peoria, Illinois

Library of Congress Cataloging-in-Publication Data
Squire, Ann, author.
 Extreme laboratories / by Ann O. Squire.
  pages cm. — (A true book)
 Audience: 9–12.
 Audience: Grade 4 to 6.
 Includes bibliographical references and index.
 ISBN 978-0-531-20741-3 (library binding : alk. paper) — ISBN 978-0-531-21552-4 (pbk. : alk. paper)
 1. Laboratories—Juvenile literature. 2. Research—Juvenile literature. I. Title.
 Q183.A1S68 2014
 507.2—dc23   2014005456

Front cover: Large Hadron Collider
Back cover: Researcher with magnifying glass

Find the Truth!

Everything you are about to read is true *except* for one of the sentences on this page.

Which one is **TRUE**?

T or F The International Space Station took more than 10 years to build.

T or F Scientists only study things that they can see.

Find the answers in this book.

Contents

THE BIG TRUTH!

A researcher photographs an underground glacier.

Astronauts use tethers to keep them attached to a spacecraft while working outside.

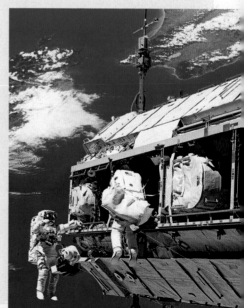

A researcher peeks out of a view port
in the underwater Aquarius Reef Base.

CHAPTER 1

What Is a Laboratory?

What do you imagine when you picture a **laboratory**? Do you see white-coated scientists surrounded by test tubes and beakers? Many laboratories do look much like this. But labs come in all shapes, sizes, and locations. Some are truly extreme. There are pyramid labs built high in the mountains and capsules deep below the sea. Other labs are tunnels located miles underground or outposts completely out of this world! But why exactly do scientists need labs?

 Scientists aboard Aquarius are sometimes called aquanauts.

Safety First

Sometimes, researchers use a lab for safety reasons. Certain chemicals and other substances can be dangerous. It would be a big mistake to do an explosive chemical experiment in your kitchen or at the dining room table. An experiment using dangerous **radiation** is also potentially harmful. Most laboratories are equipped with hoods under which potentially dangerous experiments are performed. There are also showers to wash off harmful substances, fire extinguishers, and other safety equipment.

Hoods protect a researcher from dangerous gases that might be created during an experiment.

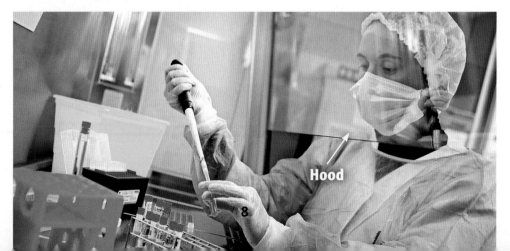

Hood

Scientific containers generally have measurement markings.

Different safety gloves are made to resist different types of chemicals.

A Controlled Environment

Another reason for working in a laboratory is that many conditions can be controlled there. Imagine doing a chemistry experiment outside in the park. You set up your chemicals and test tubes on a picnic table. You are about to mix them to see what happens. What can go wrong?

Some research must take place outside, such as in environmental studies. Scientists work to design experiments that account for any variables that might be out of their control.

Just as you start your experiment, it begins to rain. Some drops of water fall into your test tubes. Next, the wind picks up and it starts to get chilly. It is also getting dark. You have trouble seeing just how much of one chemical you are mixing with the other. The rain, the wind, the air temperature, and the lighting are all changing conditions called **variables**. They can all affect the outcome of your chemistry experiment.

Reliable Results

Working in the park, your results might be very different from one day to the next. Rainwater mixed with your chemicals can change the reaction they create. Mixing substances in the dark can leave you with too much of one or not enough of another.

Researchers must control the environment so that they control which variables change. For many experiments, the best way to do this is to carry them out in a laboratory.

Labs include a variety of instruments that help researchers make accurate measurements.

12

CHAPTER 2

Labs High and Low

For some scientists, getting to the lab is as simple as hopping in the car and driving a few miles. For others, it is much more challenging to obtain the data they need for an experiment. The Pyramid International Laboratory/Observatory is located at the base of Mount Everest in Nepal. Researchers working there have quite the trek. They must climb to an **altitude** of 16,568 feet (5,050 meters) to reach the laboratory. The entire journey can take a week!

The Pyramid sits about 12,500 feet (3,810 m) below Mount Everest's peak.

←

Lone Lab

The Pyramid houses laboratories, offices, and living quarters for visiting researchers. High in the mountains, it is very isolated from the rest of the world. As a result, the building must be completely self-sufficient. All of its energy needs are met by a large **solar power** system. Despite its isolation, researchers come from all over the world to work here. As of 2013, 220 people from 143 different institutions have done research at the Pyramid.

The Pyramid is a three-story structure made of aluminum, steel, and glass.

14

The Pyramid uses a number of different tools to monitor the atmosphere.

Weather Station

Research at the Pyramid has been vital to understanding and protecting Earth. Since the lab opened in 1990, scientists have monitored the weather, climate, and atmosphere of the mountain regions surrounding Mount Everest. They have found that air pollution is reaching even these remote areas. The pollution is affecting the snow cover on Himalayan peaks. This information is helping researchers understand how humans are affecting our planet's climate.

A sign welcomes visitors to the depths of the Sanford Lab.

Underground Lab

Far below the Black Hills of South Dakota, scientists look for clues to how our universe formed. The roughly 5,000-foot-deep (1,524 m) Sanford Underground Research Facility was built in an abandoned gold mine. There, it is shielded from the cosmic radiation naturally found in the universe. This makes the facility the perfect place to study **dark matter**, **neutrinos**, and other phenomena. These things cannot be detected in ordinary labs that experience cosmic radiation on Earth's surface.

Even Deeper

The Sanford Lab is deep. But a similar lab outside Sudbury, Ontario, Canada, is even deeper. In fact, SNOLAB is the deepest lab in the world. It is roughly 1.2 miles (2 kilometers) underground. Researchers there also study dark matter and neutrinos. Like the Sanford Lab, SNOLAB was originally a mine. The mine was turned into the Sudbury Neutrino Observatory (SNO) in the 1990s. Between 2004 and 2012, SNO was expanded to create SNOLAB.

Scientists must travel deep underground to reach SNOLAB.

Keeping It Clean

Dust can affect neutrino experiment results. Therefore, neutrino research must be done in a very clean lab. This can be difficult in a dusty mine. Every person and object must be cleaned before entering SNOLAB's research area. People shower and change into clean clothes. Some materials are cleaned directly. Other materials could be damaged by the cleaning process. These are packed into containers before being sent underground. The containers are cleaned, and then brought into the lab and opened.

Everything in **SNOLAB's** research area must be as free of dust as possible—including the air!

Getting to Work

Norway's underground Svartisen Subglacial Laboratory is tough to reach. To get there, scientists catch a flight to a remote town in the Arctic. Then they take a long drive, a ferryboat ride, and a several-hour hike along a snowy trail to the lab's tunnel entrance. After descending to 700 feet (213 m) below the ice, scientists finally reach the lab. Fortunately, there are bedrooms, a kitchen, and a bathroom. After this long trip, most researchers stay awhile!

A scientist photographs ice at the Svartisen Subglacial Laboratory.

IceCube covers a wide area and
extends deep into the ice.

CHAPTER 3

Labs Cold and Hot

One of the coldest laboratories on Earth is the Svartisen Subglacial Lab. There, scientists conduct research at the very bottom of a glacier. Another super-cold lab is found in Antarctica: the IceCube South Pole Neutrino Observatory. Temperatures there have been recorded as low as –135 degrees Fahrenheit (–93 degrees Celsius). Sensors, or devices that detect changes or activities, are buried 4,750 to 8,040 feet (1,448 to 2,450 m) deep.

About 275 million cosmic rays are detected at the IceCube lab every day.

Chasing Neutrinos

IceCube scientists are searching for neutrinos. But neutrinos are not visible. How do researchers at IceCube find them? When a neutrino interacts with an atom of ice, it produces a glowing blue light. Then one of the 5,160 basketball-size sensors buried in the ice sends a signal to the surface. The sensors record the light's strength and direction of movement. Researchers use this information to figure out where in the universe the neutrino originated.

Holes to hold IceCube's sensors are melted in the ice using a hot water drill.

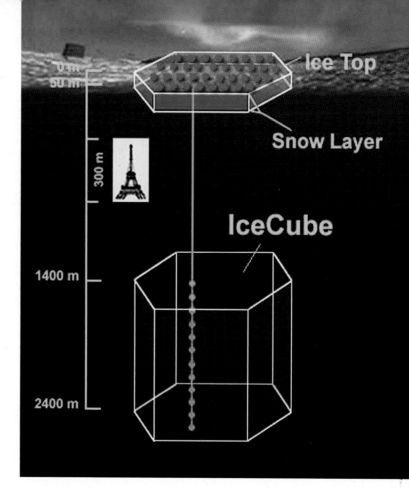

The IceCube lab building where scientists work is on the top in this illustration. Deep underground are the sensors. The Eiffel Tower is shown for scale.

The IceCube lab is not only one of the coldest labs, it is one of the largest. The neutrino detectors are buried throughout a giant chunk of ice, 0.24 cubic miles (1 cubic km) in volume. If all of this ice melted, it would produce enough water to fill one million swimming pools!

The South Pole Station includes several buildings spread over a large area.

The Bottom of the World

Antarctica does not just have neutrinos. It also has some of the cleanest air on Earth. For this reason, the National Oceanic and Atmospheric Administration (NOAA) built a lab there. The South Pole Observatory (SPO) is located exactly at Earth's South Pole. SPO researchers study changes in the climate and atmosphere. The lab was originally completed in 1957. Its research was so important and successful that the lab was improved in 1975 and 1997.

The lab supports about 150 people during the South Pole's summer months. During the winter, it supports about 50 people. In the southern half of the world, the seasons are opposite to the northern half. When it's summer in North America, it is winter in Antarctica. SPO is difficult to reach even in the summer. During the winter, it is impossible. Winter SPO staff members are on their own from mid-February through October.

People at the station operations center monitor SPO 24 hours a day all year.

The Coldest Lab in the World

Massachusetts Institute of Technology (MIT) labs are not cold. But scientists there have cooled a gas to the lowest temperature ever recorded in the universe. The gas was just barely above absolute zero. At room temperature, individual atoms move at about the speed of a jet airplane. At absolute zero, atoms do not move at all. At the super-low temperature MIT researchers caused, atoms move only about 2 inches (5 centimeters) per minute.

The Massachusetts Institute of Technology is known as a leader in scientific research.

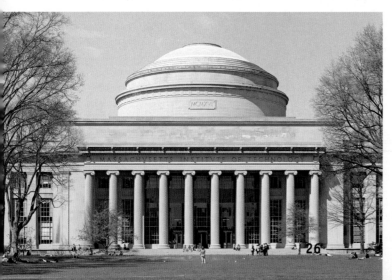

Absolute zero is -460 degrees Fahrenheit (-273 degrees Celsius).

In an experiment at Brookhaven National Laboratory, two gold particles made this pattern when they collided.

And the Hottest

Scientists at the Brookhaven National Laboratory in New York achieved the hottest temperature ever recorded. To create such heat, they smashed gold atoms together at nearly the speed of light. The energy released was 250,000 times hotter than the center of the sun. The superheated atoms formed a liquid-like substance called plasma. This hot plasma is remarkably similar to the kind that forms at super-cold temperatures. Scientists are still figuring out why this is true.

The World's Weirdest Lab

There are many unusual laboratories in the world—hot and cold, high and low. But one lab is so strange that it does not fit into any category. It is called FLIP, or FLoating Instrument Platform. This ocean research vessel was built to study such things as wave heights and water temperature.

The 355-foot (108 m) ship does a neat trick: it can be flipped to float with its nose in the air. It does this by pumping water into one end and air into the other. During the 28-minute transformation, the ship gradually tilts. Walls become the floors. Beds, toilets, stoves, and scientific instruments all swivel into new positions.

When FLIP is vertical, 300 feet (91 m) of the ship are underwater. The part above the water is as tall as a five-story building. FLIP carries a crew of five people and up to 11 researchers. During the month-long research missions, all 16 people must share just one bathroom!

Workers carefully remove a piece from a detector at the Large Hadron Collider.

CHAPTER 4

Labs Large and Small

Just outside Geneva, Switzerland, is a **physics** laboratory that takes the prize as the largest in the world. It is called CERN, or European Organization for Nuclear Research. CERN was designed to study the behavior of the universe's tiniest particles. The lab speeds up particles such as **protons** and smashes them into each other. The massive machine where this happens is the Large Hadron Collider (LHC).

The Large Hadron Collider cost more than $4 billion to build.

The yellow circle in this photograph outlines the ring of the LHC.

A Giant Circle

The LHC is an extreme machine. It is buried 328 feet (100 m) belowground. It forms a doughnut-shaped ring almost 17 miles (27 km) around. Inside are magnets powerful enough to push particles at almost the speed of light. Two particle beams travel around the ring in opposite directions, moving faster and faster. At a certain point, another magnet squeezes the particles closer together. If all goes well, particles from the two beams collide.

By studying what happens when particles collide in the LHC, researchers hope to learn more about how our universe formed. Scientists believe that, nearly 14 billion years ago, the universe began to expand from a very hot and dense state. They call the start of this expansion the Big Bang. When the tiny particles crash at the LHC, they release energy. This energy is much like what existed in our universe's first few moments.

This image shows the paths of particles after a particle collision at CERN.

Invention of the World Wide Web

More than 10,000 scientists from over 100 different countries are involved in research at CERN. To help them keep in touch, British scientist Tim Berners-Lee came up with something completely new. He created a computer-based information sharing system. In 1991, CERN released this system to the physics community. Since then, the system has become very popular. You have probably used it, even if you're not a physicist. It is called the World Wide Web!

Tim Berners-Lee still works to improve the standards of the World Wide Web.

A diver swims outside the Aquarius Reef Base.

Aquarius is built to withstand the pressure of water depths of up to 120 feet (36 m).

An Underwater Lab

One of the world's smallest labs is found in a surprising place: the ocean floor. The Aquarius Reef Base rests 60 feet (18 m) below the water's surface, just off the coast of Florida. The lab is about the length of a city bus. In that cramped space are laboratories and living quarters for up to six people. Aquarius scientists study ocean life and coral reefs. They live and work underwater for 10 days at a time.

Under Pressure

Water is heavy. Aquarius researchers experience pressures two and a half times the air pressure at the water's surface. Moving too quickly from that kind of pressure to the surface is hard on the body. Therefore, scientists undergo a full 16 hours of **decompression** at the end of every mission. The pressure inside Aquarius is gradually reduced to equal that at the surface. Then the scientists can swim to the surface without risking their health.

Researchers need to decompress only before surfacing. They can move around inside and outside Aquarius without worrying about decompression.

36

Life Support

At Aquarius, basic needs are taken care of by the Life Support Buoy (LSB). This 33-foot-wide (10 m) platform floats on the surface. The buoy has a communication tower, generators to produce power, and air compressors to provide air. A thick hose containing all the wires, cables, and air hoses links the buoy to the lab. Thanks to the LSB, Aquarius scientists have all the comforts of home, including radios and cell phones!

CHAPTER 5

A Far-Out Lab

Orbiting at an altitude of 250 miles (402 km) is the world's most far-out lab: the International Space Station (ISS). The ISS provides working and living quarters for three to six astronauts at a time. The interior space is about the size of a five-bedroom house. When you include the giant solar panels on the outside that provide power, the ISS spans an area about the size of a football field.

The ISS has been occupied continuously since November 2000.

Building the ISS

Building in space is not easy. The ISS was one of the biggest construction projects in history. The first **module** was launched on an unmanned Russian rocket in 1998. The National Aeronautics and Space Administration's (NASA) space shuttle, and spacecraft from other countries, delivered the remaining pieces. Astronauts put the pieces together in space. By the time it was finished, the ISS cost $150 billion. This made it the most expensive laboratory ever built.

A group of astronauts constructs parts of the ISS outside the station.

The ISS was not officially completed until 2011.

40

Astronaut Aki Hoshide works on equipment in an ISS lab.

Space Science

The research labs on the ISS allow scientists to investigate all kinds of things. Physics, astronomy, meteorology, and biology are just a few of the areas being studied. The ISS is also a great place to study the effects of microgravity, or weightlessness, and the space environment on the human body. Astronauts spend more than half of each day on the ISS doing research and maintaining the labs.

Daily Life

In the Space Station's weightless environment, everyday tasks require careful planning. Most food is sealed in foil packages. Astronauts are careful not to spill liquids or drop crumbs, which would float everywhere, causing a mess. Space toilets work a bit like vacuum cleaners. To bathe, astronauts usually clean themselves with moist towels. When it's time for bed, they snuggle into sleeping bags that are clipped to the wall. This keeps the astronauts from floating around during the night.

Timeline of Extreme Labs

1957
The South Pole Observatory is first completed.

1990
The Pyramid Lab opens.

1991
The World Wide Web is released to the physics community.

Spotting the Station

You can see the ISS yourself. It is visible from almost everywhere on Earth. The ISS is the third-brightest object in the sky and orbits Earth 16 times per day. NASA has a Web site that tells you when the ISS will pass over your area. To see the ISS, look for a very bright light moving from west to east. It is amazing to realize that, hundreds of miles above Earth, scientists are living and working in that far-out lab! ★

2000
Construction of the International Space Station begins.

2011
Construction of the International Space Station is completed.

2004
Workers begin expanding the Sudbury Neutrino Observatory to create SNOLAB.

Number of countries participating in the International Space Station: 15

Number of Earth orbits made by the ISS in its first 10 years of operation: 57,361

Size of the Sanford Underground Research Facility: 10,000 sq. ft. (929 sq m)

Amount of data processed by CERN computers every day: 1 petabyte, or the equivalent of 210,000 DVDs

Time it takes a proton to travel once around the Large Hadron Collider: 90 microseconds; at this speed, the proton makes 11,000 revolutions in one second

Number of atmospheric neutrinos detected by IceCube each year: about 100,000

Number of people who have conducted research at the Pyramid International Laboratory/Observatory: more than 200

Did you find the truth?

T The International Space Station took more than 10 years to build.

F Scientists only study things that they can see.

Resources

Books

Basher, Simon. *Extreme Physics*. New York: Kingfisher, 2013.

Holden, Henry M. *The Coolest Job in the Universe: Working Aboard the International Space Station*. Berkeley Heights, NJ: Enslow, 2013.

McPherson, Stephanie Sammartino. *Tim Berners-Lee: Inventor of the World Wide Web*. Minneapolis: Twenty-First Century Books, 2010.

Visit this Scholastic Web site for more information on extreme laboratories:
www.factsfornow.scholastic.com
Enter the keywords **Extreme Laboratories**

Important Words

altitude (AL-tih-tood) — the height of something above the ground or above sea level

dark matter (DARK MAT-ur) — a type of material substance that cannot be seen directly; scientists believe that dark matter makes up perhaps 90 percent of the mass of the universe

decompression (dee-kuhm-PRESH-uhn) — the release or reduction of physical pressure on something

laboratory (LAB-ruh-tor-ee) — a room or building that has special equipment for people to use for scientific experiments

module (MAH-jool) — a separate unit that can be joined to others to make things such as machines and buildings

neutrinos (noo-TREE-noz) — particles that are smaller than an atom and have no electrical charge; they are believed to have little or no mass

physics (FIZ-iks) — the science that deals with matter and energy

protons (PROH-tahnz) — the very small parts in the nucleus, or center, of an atom; protons carry a positive electrical charge

radiation (ray-dee-AY-shuhn) — atomic particles that are sent out from a radioactive substance, or a substance whose atoms are breaking down

solar power (SOH-lur POW-ur) — energy from the sun that can be used for heating or generating electricity

variables (VAIR-ee-uh-buhlz) — things that are likely to change

Index

About the Author

Ann O. Squire is a psychologist and an animal behaviorist. Before becoming a writer, she studied the behavior of rats, tropical fish in the Caribbean, and electric fish from central Africa. Her favorite part of being a writer is the chance to learn as much as she can about all sorts of topics. In addition to the Extreme Science books, Dr. Squire has written about many different animals, from lemmings to leopards and cicadas to cheetahs. She lives in Long Island City, New York.

PHOTOGRAPHS ©: Alamy Images/Jochen Tack: 2, 20; AP Images/Amber Hunt: 16; CERN: cover, 30, 32; Dreamstime/Lisa F. Young: 9; Courtesy of EvK2CNR: 12, 14, 15, 42; Getty Images: 27 (Hulton Archive), back cover (Lise Gagne); iStockphoto/skynesher: 11, 44; NASA: 41; National Geographic Creative/Brian J. Skerry: 6, 35, 36, 37; Newscom/KRT: 23; NOAA: 24; NVE/Erik Rose Johnsen: 5 top, 19; Science Source: 33 (Goronwy Tudor Jones, University of Birmingham), 38, 43 right (Roger Harris), 5 bottom, 40, 43 left; Scripps Institution of Oceanography, UC San Diego: 4, 28, 29; Shutterstock, Inc.: 34 (drserg), 26 (Jorge Salcedo); SNOLAB : 17, 18; Superstock, Inc./Mark Conlin: 10; The Image Works/Burger/Phanie: 8; USAP/Brien Barnett, National Science Foundation: 25; Wisconsin IceCube Particle Astrophysics Center/Jamie Yang, IceCube Collaboration: 22.

[9]